73-433

PR   Duff, Charles
6019   James Joyce and
.09   the plain reader
Z53
1971   Date Due

MR 25 '80			
DEC 1 3 2003			

MISSOURI BAPTIST COLLEGE LIBRARY
12542 CONWAY ROAD
ST. LOUIS, MO. 63141

 PRINTED IN U.S.A.

JAMES JOYCE AND THE PLAIN READER

JAMES JOYCE AND THE PLAIN READER

An Essay
by
CHARLES DUFF

WITH A PREFATORY LETTER
BY
HERBERT READ
Professor of Fine Art, University of Edinburgh

HASKELL HOUSE PUBLISHERS Ltd.
Publishers of Scarce Scholarly Books
NEW YORK, N. Y. 10012
1971

First Published 1932

HASKELL HOUSE PUBLISHERS LTD.
Publishers of Scarce Scholarly Books
280 LAFAYETTE STREET
NEW YORK, N. Y. 10012

73-433
Library of Congress Catalog Card Number: 78-164027

Standard Book Number 8383-1329-9

Printed in the United States of America

DEDICATED
WITHOUT MALICE TO
THE PLAIN READER

CONTENTS

	PAGE
PREFATORY LETTER BY HERBERT READ	7
JAMES JOYCE AND THE PLAIN READER	17

APPENDIX—

    (*a*) Bibliography of the Works of James Joyce . . 73

    (*b*) Criticism and Articles on Joyce . . . 74

A PREFATORY LETTER

My dear Duff,—
            It would be rather too pompous for me to write an introduction to your introduction to the work of James Joyce. A prefatory letter strikes me as more appropriate, because then I can approach the matter from a more personal point of view; and isn't your point of view, too, agreeably personal? I have before now tried to be impersonally critical about Joyce, but not with much success.

You have written your introduction for the plain reader, and it is admirably adapted for that obscure entity. All criticism should, I willingly admit, be addressed to the plain reader; but appreciation is another matter. I suspect that I appreciate Joyce for reasons which would carry little weight with any one but myself, but in saying so I have no wish to be superior. I feel very humble and not very dogmatic. What I find in Joyce may, after all, be in some sense a reflection of my own aspirations; and the reflection of an aspiration is not the solid stuff of criticism !

Joyce, as no one but Shakespeare, gives me the sense of creativeness. By this I do not mean the gross creative energy of a Balzac or a Dickens—that is an imaginative gift, outside the special province of the poet (Joyce is, of course, primarily a poet). I mean the restricted inceptive energy which is evident in a phrase, or even in a single word, rather than in a novel or a play. I can open Shakespeare at random sure of finding a fresh glitter of minted and reminted words:

And every word in it a gaping wound
Issuing life-blood

—that I find, aptly enough, on the page I have just opened. And on the same page other words such as these:

The dreadful touch of merchant-marring rocks . . .

And speak between the change of man and boy
With a reed voice . . .

Every authentic page is alive with such words.

Turn now to *Ulysses*; I open equally at random:

"His frocktails winked in bright sunshine to his fat strut."

"Stephen Daedalus watched through the webbed window the lapidary's finger prove a time-dulled chain. Dust webbed the window and the showtrays. Dust darkened the toiling fingers with their vulture nails. Dust slept on dull coils of bronze and silver, lozenges of cinnabar, or rubies, leprous and wine-dark stones."

Then take any passage from *Work in Progress*:

"Well, you know or don't you kennet or haven't I told you every telling has a taling and that's the he and the she of it. Look, look, the dusk is growing. My branches lofty are taking root. And my cold cher's gone ashley, Fieluhr? Filou! What age is at? It saon is late. 'Tis endless now since eye erewone last saw Waterhouse's clogh. They took it asunder, I hurd thum sigh. When will they reassemble it? O, my back, my back, my bach! I'd want to go to Aches-les-Pains.

Pingpong! There's the Belle for Sexaloitez!
And Concepta de Send-us-pray! Pang!
Wring out the clothes! wring in the dew!
Godavari, vert the showers! And grant thaya
grace! Aman. Will we spread them here
now? Ay, we will. Flip! Spread on your
bank and I'll spread mine on mine. Flep!
It's what I'm doing. Spread! It's churning
chill. Der went is rising. I'll lay a few
stones on the hostel sheets."

Of course, it is more than a question of words. It is a question of words in rhythmic sequence (and one day some one will write a treatise on Joyce's rhythm) and it is above all a question of the colour of words, the associations they can arouse, the fire that can be struck from them in the fury of composition. Joyce's prose is deliberately musical—one can be more precise—it shows a progressive development towards a musical form. It looks as though he early exhausted the musical possibilities of normal lyrical expression. The poems in *Chamber Music* are as purely lyrical as any in the language—for my taste they are too lyrical—the music is so melodious that the meaning is irrelevant. Of *Work in Progress* we may say what amounts to the same thing: the meaning is so obscure that just the abstracted sound of the syllables, in other words, the melody, becomes dominant.

It is arguable whether this is a legitimate development of literature. You seem to take the view that it is. But it seems to me that words must either be so abstract that they are just sound, and as such poor competitors with the sounds of normal music; or so suggestive of meaning or associations that they largely defeat their own purely musical function. To hear Joyce read his own prose (even on a gramophone record) is a remarkable revelation—a spoken opera. But opera was always a bastard type *of literature,* whatever it may be as music, and no self-respecting poet would care to see his verses reduced to the " pure " music of a *prima donna's* coloratura.

Joyce's strength rests more solidly on much more conventional grounds—on his sense of humour and his sense of character (two more qualities which he shares with Shakespeare). His humour is perhaps difficult—it is the high-horsical nonsense of a very intelligent brain, but so is *Alice in Wonderland.* It has its analogies in previous literature and in art. I came across the following passage, in one of Keats's letters the other day:

> "Here's Brown going on so that I cannot bring to mind how the last days have vanished —for example, he says: The Lady of the Lake went to Rock herself to sleep on Arthur's seat, and the Lord of the Isles coming to Press a Piece and seeing her Asleap remembered their las meeting at Corrystone Water, so touching her with one hand on the Vallis Lucis while the other unDerwent her Whitehaven, Ireby stifled her clack man on, that he might her Anglesea and give her a Buchanan and said——"

This is pretty obvious punning, you may think, but Joyce takes such a form of humour and raises it to infinite degrees of subtlety and allusiveness. And over it all he casts the spell of his musical rhythm. That subtlety or allusiveness has its literary prototype in the Anglo-Saxon *Kenning,* a once popular method of writing in riddles which may well have had its influence on Joyce. But the closest analogy to the literary method of *Work in Progress* is perhaps to be found in the early graphic art of Joyce's own country, the abstract involved ornament of the Celts. Here is a very good description of such art by a German writer:

" There are certain simple motives whose interweaving and commingling determines the character of this ornament. At first there is only the dot, the line, the ribbon; later the curve, the circle, the spiral, the zigzag, and an S-shaped decoration are employed. Truly, no great wealth of motives! But what variety is attained by the manner of their employment! Here they run parallel, then entwined, now latticed, now knotted, now plaited, then again brought through one another in a symmetrical checker of knotting and plaiting. Fantastically confused patterns are thus evolved, whose puzzle asks to be unravelled, whose convolutions seem alternatively to seek and avoid each other, whose component parts, endowed as it were with sensibility, captivate sight and sense in passionately vital movement."

If you transpose this paragraph, writing " syllables "

instead of "motives," "hearing" for "sight," you have a fairly accurate description of Joyce's developed style.

As for Joyce's sense of character, where, in modern literature, I would like to ask, have you a character with half the reality of Bloom? Joyce's method is finally justified by its success in this respect. Little by little, we can hardly realize how, this tremendous figure is built up, till he becomes as significant as Hamlet or Faust. Bloom is the emanation of a racial unconscious, a symbol of all that repressed world in man which Freud calls the Id. In this sense, *Ulysses* is the most wholesome purgative that has been offered to mankind for more than a century. That it should be banned and burnt by the public hangman is a mad example of the way mankind refuses salvation.

It is because, finally, Joyce's work becomes an expression of the unconscious (or perhaps, more Freudianly speaking, the preconscious), that it is difficult to be impersonally critical about it. One either accepts or rejects the Freudian hypothesis. I accept it, and therefore do not find it difficult to accept (and enjoy) the prose art of Joyce: but I

A PREFATORY LETTER

realize that it is difficult to rationalize my own acceptance of this art in the terms of a critical science. Joyce's later work demands a more intuitive attitude towards literature. The normal process of representative meaning followed by emotional reaction is avoided. What you have instead is a process of image-release followed by intuitive recognition. The images (and I use the word in a wide sense to include not only visual imagery, but even single words charged with associative imagery) rise to the surface of the conscious mind and are given, or take on, pattern and rhythm; the reader receives this charged stream into his conscious mind, and because, if I may mix my metaphors, it rings the bells in his preconscious or perhaps unconscious mind, he gets his thrill, he recognizes the forces of the stream, submits to its music, accepts its art.

Work in Progress may be, in Valéry Larbaud's words which you quote, an abuse of language. In the same way it might be said that the pictures of Paul Klee and Max Ernst, which offer a perfect analogy to the method of *Work in Progress,* are an abuse of paint. But every method which breaks new ground must be an abuse; you could no more give an adequate æsthetic representation of the unconscious world in the style of Edgar Wallace or Sir Frank Dicksee, R.A., than you could give an adequate scientific representation of the cosmic world by rule of thumb. The problem which Joyce attempts to solve *demands* an abuse of the literary medium; we need only ask whether Joyce's particular invention is the right one, and perhaps more fundamentally whether the problem is one which should be solved. It seems to me that your pamphlet gives a complete answer to these questions, so, without more ado, I commend it to the reader.

Yours very sincerely,

HERBERT READ.

Edinburgh, 1932.

JAMES JOYCE AND THE PLAIN READER

§ I

JAMES JOYCE'S *Anna Livia Plurabelle* has been reprinted several times since it was made available in a popular form,[1] and the publishers have followed it up with *Haveth Childers Everywhere*, another even more puzzling extract from the unfinished *Work in Progress*. When *Anna Livia* was offered to the general public, I asked myself how many people would buy it and, having bought it, how many would be capable of forming any idea of what it was all about. I have myself read it several times and still find in it words, sentences, and even paragraphs which completely baffle me, but have been inclined to attribute this to a slow-paced intellect or lack of knowledge which always makes me feel a little out of countenance when I hear people stating, with a fine show of confidence,

[1] *Criterion Miscellany* (Faber & Faber, London; 1s. net).

that there is not much in it which they do not "follow quite well."

My relief was profound when I received the *Nouvelle Revue Française* of May 1931, and realized the system or procedure followed in the translation of *Anna Livia* into French. The piece was approached as if it were, say, a precious fragment from an ancient, obscure, and important language. A round-table conference of skilled translators,[1] presided over by the author of the extract, sat upon it for several weeks, and after much labour produced a French version which the editor of the *Nouvelle Revue Française* submitted to his readers. Now for it, thought I. If the English is puzzling, there will surely be no great difficulty with the French. English is a delightfully vague language, capable of magnificent amphibologies and high-sounding anacolutha. French tends to be sharp and lucid, and it has a knack of pinning down meanings. My old French professor brought me up on the tag: *Ce qui n'est pas clair, n'est pas français.* The translation in question must be perfect, or that fastidious craftsman-linguist Joyce would not pass it. Praise God, we shall now be able to fathom the depths of *Anna Livie Plurabelle* !

Alas ! after reading the French version, I found

[1] They were: Samuel Beckett, Alfred Perron, Paul L. Léon, Adrienne Monier, Eugène Jolas, and Ivan Goll.

the enigma to be almost as far from complete solution as before: almost, because about a score of words in the " French " seemed to be a little more comprehensible than their " English " equivalents. Emotions had to take precedence over reason in order to get pleasure from either the one or the other.

It was not until *Anna Livia* reached my mind via the *ear* that I could honestly bring myself to regard it as a serious contribution to literature. Joyce's recorded [1] reading caused my doubts to disappear. The effect of speaking it aloud was almost magical. The piece seemed to me (and to one or two of my friends who had been hitherto hostile to Joyce) to free itself from the shackles of the printed word and take wings, transporting the listener to a spacious fairyland in which the imagination is thrilled by surprise after surprise. Others who have heard the record now feel as I do about it—that it provides justification for Joyce's remarkable attempt to make language do much more of the work of music than any one has ever believed to be possible. On the strength of this (to me) delightful discovery I sat down and re-read all of *Work in Progress* that has appeared in *transition,* and put it away with the firm conviction that Joyce has provided us with a chart,

[1] The Orthological Institute, Cambridge, has made this gramophone record available to the public.

a rough one perhaps, but a chart all the same, to an intellectual and spiritual ocean of almost infinite possibilities.

At this point the plain reader may ask, " But where do *I* come in? I am really quite satisfied with the masterpieces of straightforward fiction which flow from a host of pens nowadays, and are *proclaimed* to be masterpieces by a host of admirable reviewers. So why should I risk cramps in the cranium by worrying about Joyce?" All I can say in reply is that I believe the plain reader to be more intelligent than the majority of reviewers think he is, or than he suspects himself. I have been listening with malicious pleasure to what some plain readers are saying about the opinions of " reviewers " and the quality of some of those " masterpieces " ! And it is in the hope that many plain readers will be glad to have, in a convenient and easily comprehensible form, a guide to something better that these lines are written.

That some such guide is necessary I do not doubt. A writer of distinction whom I know recently denounced *Anna Livia Plurabelle* to me as sheer nonsense and declared *Ulysses* to be inexplicable and boring. His attitude towards all Joyce's work is somewhat similar to that of the eminent judge who declared solemnly that the *Midsummer Night's*

Dream is a tissue of falsehood and improbabilities from beginning to end! It struck me very forcibly that if such a man (and no doubt there are many like him) fails at this time of day to see anything in Joyce, what of the plain reader? Are *Anna Livia Plurabelle* and *Haveth Childers Everywhere* purchased as literary freaks and laughing stocks? Is *Ulysses* often bought and kept merely because it is a forbidden book? Or because of the scatological and sexual passages? Are they all bought as a sop to the intellectual snobbery of their purchasers? Do the possessors of these books realize their significance? We must assume, because of the considerable sales of *Anna Livia* and *Ulysses,* that they have reached a public well outside the comparatively small section of Joycean devotees or experts in letters—that, in short, both books are at last beginning to penetrate the strongholds of the plain reader. We must, I think, also assume that as time goes on they will reach a still wider public—though one doubts if they can ever reach a popularity approaching that of the works of our suggestive romantics, knock-about erotics, or tosh merchants. And we must hope that the more they are read and pondered over, the more chance they have of ultimate elucidation.

It is with the plain reader in mind that what

follows is written; it constitutes an effort to help him over the worst obstacles. Several attempts have been made already to explain or appraise *Ulysses*, the most expansive study hitherto being that of Stuart Gilbert [1] which, because it was written under the supervision of Joyce, is of great value. To that work must go the plain reader who does not happen to possess or have access to a full text of *Ulysses*. Far less successful efforts have been made to criticize and elucidate the unfinished *Work in Progress*. The ground has all been surveyed, but some of it very roughly, so it can do little harm to run over it again briefly and, wherever possible, draw attention to features which have been missed or completely ignored by those who have gone before. Joyce is by no means an easy writer to follow. He is so great an artist and he now occupies so high a place not merely in our own, but possibly in the whole of literature, that an apology is hardly needed for what follows. On the Continent he is accepted by critics as the type of genius to be found once in a century or in an age. Many English critics have conceded him a place amongst the giants. Why, then, should we not try to understand his work?

[1] James Joyce's *Ulysses: A Study*, by Stuart Gilbert (Faber & Faber). See also the Appendix to this essay.

§ II

Some knowledge of the principal facts of Joyce's life are necessary if any headway is to be made. All writers are autobiographical, but few more so than he—his life gives a characteristic tinge to every page. Therefore, let us first glance at his history, and consider briefly those parts of it which are of special interest.

Joyce was born in Dublin, in 1882, of Irish parents; and he was "born a Catholic." His mind is abnormally Irish—that is to say, he has the qualities which make up the typically Irish mind, but in over-developed forms. He suffers from (or is gifted with) mental gigantism of Irishness, and I think this must be our first rough pointer to his psychology. Now, the characteristic qualities of Southern Irish mentality are a restless and often fantastic imagination, a keen sense of realism and the comic, and a tendency to sombre, mystical brooding, which often finds compensation in either genial or sardonic wit. There is, furthermore, a marked loquacity and resourcefulness in the use of language, and an amazingly keen time-sense ("the Irish never will forget" is a phrase that used to be heard in England). One has merely to open at almost any page the works of, say, Swift, Berkeley,

Burke, Yeats, Moore, or Shaw to find striking illustrations of the qualities I have mentioned, and it is a strange fact that the Irish mentality is highly contagious—people of almost any race living in Ireland quickly catch it. Even the Jews are not immune from it. As to the use of language, this often becomes a sheer obsession—see, for example, Joyce's latest work; and in George Moore we have a standing example of a writer completely run to seed in this respect. For Moore, the way of saying a thing became of so great importance that the value of many of his later pages lies only in the mellifluous sound of the prose; in the matter there is often little or no substance to appeal to the intellect.

Of Joyce's mind the most noticeable qualities are its broodiness, and with this an intense language-(or perhaps) craftsmanship-obsession, in the employment of which he has shown distinct originality and a freshness rarely found amongst his contemporaries. As for his Roman Catholicism, whether we wish or not, we cannot ever get away from it—his reaction against Rome has been so violent that in this alone is to be found the dynamics behind many of his short stories, the whole of *The Portrait*, large slices of *Ulysses*, and of parts of *Work in Progress*. Like many Roman Catholics who have

JAMES JOYCE AND THE PLAIN READER

discarded their religion, Joyce seldom misses an opportunity for blasphemous ridicule, and, as he is exceptionally resourceful in the use of language and deeply learned in Church matters, his considered blasphemies are apt to horrify any plain reader who has the least respect for Latin Christianity. The good Roman Catholic who reads him requires disinfection afterwards, if the Joycean darts are not to leave septic lacerations. This explains the rough manner in which Joyce's works are handled by some critics who are conscientious Roman Catholics; it also explains why they are regarded as abominations by the Irish Free State Government.[1] Not that his treatment of other religions is any more respectful, for he regards all cults from a coldly anthropological standpoint, and this makes his writings unacceptable to the older generation of English people, to many Americans, and to puritans and hypocrites everywhere. This arrogant lack of respect for established religion on the part of Joyce has not been entirely wasted upon the men and women of a war generation who, if anything, are inclined to regard a disdain for religion as something of a virtue. (I have myself

[1] It is chiefly the Irish Roman Catholics who object to Joyce's works. The Irish R.C.'s are essentially puritan, unlike their continental co-religionists. The latter have treated all Joyce's works most generously.

been amused by prayers before battle, and disgusted with hymns afterwards. But that by the way.)

A fact often overlooked by those who attempt to appraise Joyce's work is that his education was not entirely Roman Catholic. True, his schooling was received from the Jesuits; but one ought never to forget that it was while *still with them* that he lapsed into thoroughgoing paganism. Nevertheless, the Jesuit training has been of great practical value to him as a writer. He received a grounding in scholastic philosophy, grammar, rhetoric, and dialectic, and absorbed knowledge of these subjects so rapidly that at one time he was considered by his mentors to be a very promising candidate for the Society of Jesus. But God did not call him, and without a call he refused to enter the Society. The plunge into paganism was not to his advantage in a worldly sense. From almost every point of view, except that of the artist desiring intellectual freedom, his subsequent career was entirely unsatisfactory. Thereafter he led a penurious, if picturesque, existence. At the old (and very Roman Catholic) Royal University in Dublin the path of those who refused to wear conventional intellectual spectacles was not made easier by the refusal. We read that young Joyce became quite a notorious person, a speaker at debates always willing to split hairs with

JAMES JOYCE AND THE PLAIN READER

any one. He was even outside the strong local literary movement, though deeply interested in literature. About that time he wrote an essay on the Irish Literary Theatre for the University Magazine, but it so outraged the authorities that they refused to allow it to be printed. Nothing daunted, he published the little work in 1901, in pamphlet form, and in company with an essay by Sheehy Skeffington. It is the earliest published work of his extant; another pamphlet on Parnell, said to have been written at the age of nine, is unobtainable. Joyce's political views constituted another obstacle to his popularity. He was evolving ideas regarding the social obligations of the artist, and already they pointed decisively to a complete political neutrality. On this there could be for him no sort of compromise. In such circumstances life in the Royal University would have been unpleasant for anybody; to a highly sensitive man it must have been unbearable. In this atmosphere Joyce worked at the subjects which interested him, literature and languages, and in these he made rapid progress. One of his side-efforts was to learn Norwegian and read Ibsen in the original—an achievement which, in itself, would have made him an odd freak in any Irish University. He was steadily assuming an intellectual independence amounting to arrogance, and it put him outside the pale of all movements. We often see it stated that Joyce is one of the figures thrown up by the Irish literary revival, but this is true only in the sense that he was a reaction *against* it. It is entirely erroneous to associate him in any other way with the general tendencies shown in the work of contemporary Irishmen, most of which was propagandist and therefore contrary to his whole conceptions of art. He gathered most of his literary ideas from the Continent, and yet his work is not in the least like that of any one continental writer. In *Dubliners* there are signs of the influence of Flaubert and Chechov, without the cold metallic finish of the one, or the depressing power of the other. The verse of *Chamber Music* is English and seventeenth century. *Exiles* is a reflection of Ibsen. *Ulysses* seems to contain samples of every style under the sun, and *Work in Progress* is written in a composite style which has no counterpart in language. Joyce's *literary* outlook, his craftsmanship, and philosophy became neither Irish nor English, but pan-European. This is one reason why most of his work is disconcerting to a person reading it for the first time, and especially to the plain reader. Add to literary pan-Europeanism that gigantism of Irishness already mentioned, and we know more or less what we may expect.

Between the Royal University period and the publication of *Ulysses* in 1922, Joyce's life appears to have been similar in its great variety to that of many gifted Irishmen who do not fit into a snug corner at home. He taught languages in various branches of the Berlitz School; he entered Paris University as a medical student; he studied music and began seriously to train his excellent tenor voice; he wandered from place to place on the Continent, and to and from Dublin; he married at the age of twenty-two; he wrote gentle little lyrics and planned ambitious literary works; for a while he directed the Volta cinema in Dublin; he fought against failing eyesight, struggling to make ends meet, and to maintain an appearance of respectability (for nowhere is it so important to show respectability as in Dublin). All the time he brooded, a lonely "unsuccessful" man without settled ideas of settling down. To say that these meandering efforts represented so much time wasted would be quite untrue for, being more intelligent than the average man and gifted with a prodigious, even astounding, memory, his mind was filling itself with all sorts of knowledge which he afterwards magnificently poured into *Ulysses*. The gynæcological virtuosity of the section in that book dealing with Mina Purefoy's confinement, for example, could only have been written by a student of medicine, and by one who had not missed much of importance concerning childbirth. So with the other sections; they are saturated with miscellaneous knowledge and erudition.

Joyce's collected verse was published in 1907 under the title *Chamber Music,* and an appropriate one it is. They are pleasing, dreamy little pieces, of considerable technical merit as parodies or reflections of later Elizabethan poetry, but hardly capable of either stimulating the intellect or probing the emotions. They are lyrics of the "Welladay! Welladay!" and "Hey nonny-nonny" kind. The collection of short stories known as *Dubliners,* though mostly written shortly after that period, was not published until 1914. The passions and feelings that spring from sex and religion and the dismal realities of life and death form the basis of all his themes; the setting is the frowsty, middle-class atmosphere of the Irish capital, relieved here and there by passages of comical or ironical reaction. Some of the stories in *Dubliners* are little gems of word-painting in which the author uses a Defoe-like style, pleasing alike to plain reader and purist. In this book Joyce began to apply the Flaubertian naturalistic method, lightly, and with some reticence, as if he were not quite sure of himself.

Already he was showing a determination to face the facts of life, reflecting them as faithfully as his ability would permit, and without the least regard for conventional ideas of ethics or for susceptibilities, or the slightest consideration for public taste. One story, " The Dead," is, so far as I know, unique in English literature; a mystical probing of the mind in the presence of death, comparable to passages in the *Guia espiritual* of the seventeenth-century Spaniard Miguel de Molinos, founder of Quietism, with whom Joyce has much in common. The next book, *A Portrait of the Artist as a Young Man,* was published in 1916. It describes the education of Stephen Dedalus by the Jesuits, his revolt against Roman Catholicism, the formation of his artist mind, and the evolution of the artistic creed which was to replace religion. The mind of the artist must be " *arrested and raised above desire and loathing.*" The words italicized provide an explanation of the " obscenity," irreligion, and disrespect for conventions to be found in *Ulysses,* which was then being written. They explain why Joyce thinks it essential for the artist to be frank: to hold back *anything* that pertains to life he regards as a sign of insincerity, dishonesty, or incompetence. By merely refusing to point a moral or to write to provide mental soporifics, by refusing to consider for a moment any readers but those whose minds are untrammelled by religion, politics, or social inhibitions of any sort, by using a technique most apt for his purpose, and by presenting not merely the externals of life but the most minute mental reactions of his characters to them, Joyce undoubtedly extended the scope of the novel. He gave it a new turn, which was a complete breakaway from sentimentalism, the abomination of propaganda, and the shoddy " kinetic " art of so many contemporary novelists. In other words, he showed the novelists how they failed as creative artists by giving the public what it wanted. Other writers have attempted to do this, but the glory of being the first to do it on the heroic scale is his. *The Portrait* is an interesting work in the history of the technique of the novel, but both it and *Dubliners* pale into insignificance in comparison with the immense conception and wonderful execution of *Ulysses*. The play *Exiles* I mention only to dismiss, perhaps a little too summarily. I have not seen it acted, and therefore cannot judge of its value as a play. It is written in a simple, direct style; it has a commonplace double-triangular plot; and the traditional rules of three-act-play technique are carefully observed. But it falls very flat in the reading and, had it not been written by so great an artist as James

Joyce, I doubt if it would attract much attention. It is Ibsenish without Ibsen's fine sense of drama.

To *Ulysses*, the banned book, we must go for Joyce's greatest contribution to literature. *Work in Progress* is unfinished and cannot yet be judged. But *Ulysses* is without doubt an outstanding achievement of the human mind, a monumental work of art. Toddling in *Dubliners*, walking with unfaltering steps in *The Portrait*, Joyce seems to have become possessed of seven-leagued boots in *Ulysses*. It adds something to man's knowledge of himself. After having read it we feel that we have been not merely in the presence of the characters, but actually inside their minds. We know them better than we know our most intimate friends. Leopold Bloom is an immortal figure; and there is no woman in literature to equal Marion.

§ III

The story or plot of Joyce's *Ulysses* is simple enough in outline. It is a narrative of the events of a typical Dublin day, June 16th, 1904, in so far as they came within the orbit of the lives of certain characters, especially Stephen Dedalus, Leopold Bloom, and his wife Marion Bloom. The spiritual or symbolical significance of these and the minor personalities in the book will be mentioned later, but it is important that the plain reader should learn at the earliest possible moment some general idea of the framework around which Joyce erects his elaborate, Dantesque edifice. He himself attaches inordinate importance to his carefully chosen literary device of making the various episodes of the day correspond with the episodes of Homer's *Odyssey*. But this conceit, it seems to me, is unnecessarily laboured. Either the events happened in the manner or order in which they are given, or they did not; if they did, well and good. We realize very soon that Stephen Dedalus (usually taken to be Joyce himself) corresponds to Telemachus, that the Jew Leopold Bloom is Ulysses the *wanderer*, and that other characters and events more or less tally with those in the *Odyssey*, but these facts in themselves do not add one whit to a recorded experience that is magnificently able to stand on its own legs. I had read the book twice with enjoyment, and, I believe, some understanding, before I bothered to look closely at the Homeric clothes-line upon which that huge heap of dirty Dublin linen is spread out before us. We may well leave it for learned commentators to amuse themselves with, and assume that the plain reader need not worry too much about it. If he cannot

JAMES JOYCE AND THE PLAIN READER

appreciate the book without it, he will never do so with it; though he may find amusement piecing together the *Odyssey*-Joyce jigsaw puzzle.

Ulysses opens with an account of a rather pointless conversation between "stately plump Buck Mulligan" (*Antinous*) and the twenty-two year old Stephen Dedalus (*Telemachus*) in a Martello tower in which they are living outside Dublin. They are joined by Haines, "a ponderous Saxon" and conceited bore, who is Stephen's intellectual inferior and not nearly as pleasant a fellow as the rough and hearty Mulligan. But Haines, being of a race "bursting with money and indigestion," is often financially helpful to the two irresponsibles—hence they tolerate his presence, even if they both inwardly detest him. The first (or *Telemachus*) episode consists chiefly of the banal and inconsequential sort of conversation one might expect to hear amongst a trio consisting of a dreamy and feckless poet-schoolmaster, a rumbustious though by no means witless Dublin "bucko," and a tiresome Englishman whose Oxford culture enables him to pass off a natural stodginess as something precious and unattainable by the two members of an inferior though untamable breed. The scene changes for the second (or *Nestor*) episode, and here we find Stephen teaching a class of brats at Mr.

Deasy's school. He is not uninterested in his task but, in the manner of many imaginative men of all races, and especially the Irish, he is inclined to dash off at attractive tangents and forget all about the serious work of the moment. The boys are fond of him, though they regard him as the sort of person whose leg can be well pulled without risk of danger. Thus, in the middle of the lesson one of them asks him to tell them a story, an idea immediately taken up by another who suggests that it be a ghost story. A moment later the work is forgotten while the master asks his class riddles! It is altogether a very Dublin classroom atmosphere, and the time is whiled away with harmless exchanges of wit and wisdom until the hour of freedom strikes. Serious work finished, Stephen goes to Mr. Deasy's study. It is the monthly pay-day, and Mr. Deasy hands over the three pounds twelve shillings with some unctuous moralizing in the manner of Samuel Smiles, which nauseates Stephen. Emphasis is laid by Deasy upon the pride of the English in paying their way. Could Stephen say that he did as much? Could he put his hand on his heart and say that he owed nothing? Alas, no! He runs over in his mind a list of debts: Mulligan, nine pounds; Curran, ten guineas; McCann, a guinea, etc., etc., not to mention five weeks' board

JAMES JOYCE AND THE PLAIN READER

owing to his landlady. The sum of money he has just received is useless to meet a fraction of his debts. He is worried and disgusted and, in this frame of mind, wanders off to the beach to think things over. In the beach (or *Proteus*) episode we are introduced to the special technique which Joyce has used throughout *Ulysses* with remarkable effect: the simultaneous presentation to the reader of the mental processes and reactions of the character and the events of the physical world around him. We see, as it were, two pictures, and of the two the one of the psychological processes is very often (as in this instance) the more impressive. The hard naturalism of Flaubert is applied to the painting of a vivid picture of the stream of consciousness. Nothing is omitted of those incoherencies and inconsequentialities which are interspersed in a seemingly haphazard manner amongst the directed thoughts or musings of perfectly sane people. The technique of this "silent monologue" is not new.[1] It is at least as old as Shakespeare; Wyndham Lewis has shown us how Dickens used it in *Pickwick*. Dorothy Richardson came close to it, but Joyce claims to have taken the idea from Dujardin's novel, *Les Lauriers sont coupés,* now a literary curiosity

[1] In *Le Correspondant,* No. 1664, of 25th January 1932, M. Daniel-Rops gives an interesting account of this *Monologue intérieur.*

because it was the forerunner of the technical method which provides so much of the power of *Ulysses*. Wherever it comes from, there is one thing certain: no writer either before or after *Ulysses* has used the silent monologue half so effectively as Joyce or, at the same time, in a manner more likely to baffle and dismay the plain reader in his first attempts to grapple with the book. Until the trick is fully appreciated, pages of *Ulysses* are literary nightmare. They are likely to drive all but the stoutest to despair. Take one of the simplest examples from the beach episode:

> " Airs romped around him, nipping and eager airs. They are coming, waves. The whitemaned seahorses champing, brightwind-bridled, the steeds of Mananaan.
> " I mustn't forget his letter for the press. And after? The ship, half twelve. By the way go easy with that money like a good young imbecile. Yes I must.
> " His pace slackened. Here. Am I going to Aunt Sara's or not? My consubstantial father's voice. Did you see anything of your artist brother Stephen lately? No?"

Here it is comparatively plain sailing. But the further we get into the book the more difficult it becomes, and there are occasions—the *Sirens* episode, for example—when even the most sophisticated reader finds it so complicated that to grasp the meaning at all a considerable intellectual effort is necessary, a complete recollection of dozens of trivial incidents that have gone before; also comprehension of a number of allusions (obscure except to scholars), and in addition some familiarity with Dublin life of the period ! It is like reading the *Odyssey* itself in this respect. No wonder, therefore, that the book is frequently put away by many a plain reader never to be reopened. Nor is it any wonder that when those who persist in their struggle with the book discover that, far from being nonsense, it achieves beautifully what it sets out to do, they are lost in admiration, and can re-read it again and again with enjoyment.

Up to the beach episode, then, the story is comparatively straightforward, if a little dull. The style is pure, though hardly of exceptional merit. In the beach episode it rises suddenly to a higher level, which taxes the reader's intelligence and demands a closer attention, but at the same time it begins to grip his imagination forcibly. If we had not done so before we now begin to get an insight into the mind and character of the dreamy, unhappy Dedalus; henceforward our interest in him seldom flags. By the time he has finished this third episode (which also ends Part I of the book) the reader may well decide that *Ulysses* is not for him; or, if he has seen through the technical tricks and grasped their significance and possibilities, he needs little persuasion to go on.

The time occupied so far is from 8 a.m. to 11 a.m., and there is nothing during this period which Stephen has done except breathe with which we have not been made fully acquainted. An amount of space approximately the equivalent of one half of that of an average modern novel is taken to describe a few minor events in the life of a character during a period of three hours by the clock.

§ IV

We leave Stephen sitting brooding on the beach, wrapped in his thoughts as he looks at a passing ship and, in the opening of Part II, we are introduced to the next very important character—Leopold Bloom, aged thirty-eight, an advertising tout. Bloom is in many ways a typical Dublinized Roman Catholic Jew; but we shall see later that there is more in him than that. The scene of this (*Calypso*) episode is in his house where, beginning again at eight o'clock on the same morning, we find him preparing breakfast for his wife Marion and himself. Marion Bloom is the third great character—"the woman of the piece." As her husband walks about the kitchen making tea and " righting her breakfast things on the bumpy tray" we are taken within his mind to find him discussing with himself the gastronomic qualities of grilled kidneys. His is a mixture of Irish and Jewish minds—semi-oriental, imaginative, materialistic, and sensuous. His speech and mannerisms are unmistakably Dublin. He informs Marion, as she dozes in bed, that he is going out to buy kidneys for breakfast. We are taken with him through the streets to the butcher's, and while he contemplates the attractions of a girl customer with whom he would gladly become acquainted. But courage fails him, so he returns home, grills a kidney, slaps it on a plate, and brings Marion her breakfast in bed—a significant act on his part, we find later; it is the first time in ten years that he has done this, for it is she who usually waits upon him.

Little by little we learn that Marion is a trull, a practitioner of infidelity on the grand scale. Her sexual appetite is, apparently, incapable of being satisfied, hence Bloom is not known as Bloom but as Marion Bloom's husband—such is her notoriety. She is by profession a singer, but hardly a diva in ability. By birth she is the offspring of a garrison officer at Gibraltar and a Spanish wench. That morning she had received a letter from her latest flame, a flashy singer-adventurer named Blazes Boylan. Bloom knows about Marion's affair with Boylan, and he is suspicious of the letter; however, she puts him off ingeniously. The relations between the two have not been satisfactory since the death of their only son Rudy many years previously. Neither has quite recovered from the shock of the tragedy: to his Jewish pride and to her maternal instincts it was a severe blow. The event marked the beginning of both their infidelities—hers unrestrained, his on a mean, petty, and carefully planned level, prompted by that Dublin hypocrisy which is narrower than its equivalent elsewhere. After some strained conversation between the two, we are made to attend on Bloom while he solemnly and in a long-drawn-out manner performs the ceremony of the cloaca. In the description of this there is no attempt to shirk the responsibilities which fall upon the author. He has taken upon himself to provide a description, painstaking and exhaustive, of the events of the day; and the cloacal event could very easily be dismissed in a few words or (in the manner of the conventional novelist) left out altogether, to be assumed by the reader. Such

JAMES JOYCE AND THE PLAIN READER

a slipshod and inartistic method makes no appeal to Joyce. Bloom must visit the jakes and, as he has been suffering from slight constipation, he expects to sit there patiently for a little while. Therefore he takes with him *Tit-Bits* to read, etc. etc. We are given over two pages of matter redolent of the privy. This is mentioned so that the plain reader shall be in no doubt as to what he must face if he wishes to read *Ulysses*. Joyce not merely holds up the mirror to nature, but at times he places in front of it a magnifying glass, and he who is not prepared to read many thoroughly " unpleasant " passages ought not to read the book at all. Let me make one point clear. The description of the above event is in perfect proportion as regards both the time and space given to it—no more and no less. It is inserted in a coldly intellectual manner, without the slightest sign of any attempt by the author to gloat over what might easily, in less competent hands, become a piece of calculated coprology. Remember that the mind of the artist must be " *arrested and raised above desire and loathing,*" and you will find that this is exactly what is happening in Joyce's descriptions of unpleasant aspects of the life of his characters. Joyce's mind is not dirty, as I believe Bernard Shaw has stated. It is as clean as the average, but it is devastatingly honest.

Bloom goes out to call at a Post Office, where he collects a letter addressed to him in another name by the lady with whom he is at present diverting himself. He pockets it, wanders through the streets, chats with an acquaintance, wanders on, and, attracted by music, casually slips into a church. Besides, he tells himself, church is a "nice discreet place to be next to some girl." All this time the action is negligible; but Bloom's mind is continuously before us. As with Stephen Dedalus on the beach, we are always in this (the *Lotus Eaters*) episode inside it.

After the church visit, which has not provided the slightest sexual titillation, he visits a public bath where he washes and tidies himself in preparation for the next (*Hades*) episode—to him the most important event of the day, namely, attendance at the funeral of his friend the late Mr. Patrick Dignam. The description of Dignam's funeral is a superb piece of reporting, one of the best things in the book. An under-current of bitterly sardonic humour runs through it, and there must be something wrong with the sense of humour of the reader who does not find it laughable. Bloom though ostensibly a Roman Catholic, by race a Jew, and baptized a Protestant, is now a would-be "progressive" with leanings towards science and free-thinking which he never attempts to conceal. Indeed, he misses no opportunity of parading his advanced opinions, which generally cause either boredom or disgust in those around him. Yet, there are moments during the impressive service for the burial of the dead when he is assailed by doubts. Those moments of grave-side emotion are obliterated or counterbalanced by the most blasphemous and callous reaction. The funeral well over, he next makes his way to the office of the *Freeman's Journal,* in which the next (*Æolus*) episode is staged. Here the text of the narrative is divided into sections under journalistic headlines: they begin conventionally, but become more and more like those of the yellow press until, in the end, they surpass in slick vulgarity and slanginess the worst taste imaginable. Throughout the episode there is a multiple appeal to the senses, masterly and convincing. Journalistic shop-talk is mixed with high-falutin' arguments; the roar of printing presses, the smell of printers' ink and news-print come and go in sharp spasms as doors are opened or closed; the vague noise of traffic can be heard through the open windows; telephone calls, proof correction, and the whole gamut of newspaper activities break in on the conversation which continually shifts from subject to subject. This episode is also noteworthy for a slight advance in plot:

Leopold Bloom and Stephen Dedalus meet for the first time, but the encounter appears to have little significance. One thing may strike the reader: both characters are now in a similar mood. They are both gloomy and dissatisfied with life—Stephen because of his debts, his intellectual discontent, and memories of his mother's death, of which the anniversary recurred only a few days before; and Bloom because the funeral has depressed him, and because he cannot drive away thoughts of the scandalous infidelities of his whorish wife. In Stephen's mind there is a struggle between a rapidly growing rationalism, which is ousting the faith inculcated by the mother he loved so deeply and whose tenets he promised on her deathbed to fulfil. The deep unhappiness and perplexities of the two men show themselves casually but unmistakably from time to time. Bloom goes out for lunch, and this event is made an episode (the *Lestrygonians*) in itself. He enters a cheap eating-house, and from the description, I take a passage to illustrate the style:

> "His heart astir he pushed in the door of the Burton restaurant. Stink gripped his trembling breath: pungent meatjuice, slop of greens. See the animals feed.

" Men, men, men.

" Perched on high stools by the bar, hats shoved back, at the tables calling for bread no charge, swilling, wolfing gobfulls of sloppy food, their eyes bulging, wiping wetted moustaches. A pallid suetfaced young man polished his tumbler, knife, fork, and spoon with his napkin. New set of microbes. A man with an infant's saucestained napkin tucked round him, shovelled gurgling soup down his gullet. A man spitting back on his plate : halfmasticated gristle : no teeth to chewchewchew it. Chump chop from the grill. Bolting to get it over. Sad booser's eyes. Bitten off more than he can chew. Am I like that? See ourselves as others see us," etc. etc.

The place was more than Bloom could stand, so he backs out and goes to Davy Byrne's quiet little " pub." A revolt against the animalism of the other foul place drives him to select a fastidious little snack-lunch, after which he goes to the public library to look up an old advertisement. Dedalus happens to be there already, discussing literature with a few Dublin " highbrows," whose real names are given. He and Bloom do not meet. This next episode (*Scylla and Charybdis*) consists almost entirely of literary discussions, and they are hardly likely to interest the plain reader. He is almost sure to find them terribly dull. Stephen endeavours without great success to clarify his ideas on *Hamlet*. Nothing is proved to anybody's satisfaction; and the whole of this part is on a level of sombre intellectualism. There is, however, a piece of cliché lewdness just towards the end which enlivens it.

In the next episode (*The Wandering Rocks*) we reach the centre of the book. It will be remembered that the time-beginning was at 8 a.m.; the time-end is something after 2 a.m. the following morning; the dramatic climax is at midnight. Thus, even in a time-sense *The Wandering Rocks*, in which the time is from 3 p.m. to 4 p.m., is approximately half way through the whole work. Everywhere Joyce observes each tick of the clock.

We are now taken through the Dublin streets, of which a score of incidents are described: commonplace happenings, conversations overheard, notabilities and notorieties seen, and so forth. Stephen and his father, Simon Dedalus, again appear; also Buck Mulligan and a number of other characters, some of whom have not appeared hitherto, and others who will not reappear, except in the phantasmagoria staged in the brothel. The Lord Lieutenant drives from the Viceregal Lodge followed by a cavalcade. These incidents are intended to give, and succeed admirably in giving, us a strong breath of the street atmosphere of Dublin on that typical June day in the year 1904. The score of apparently unrelated happenings provides a panoramic background for the mental and spiritual spectrum-analysis of the more important characters—a process which begins early in the first chapter and ends with the superb, unparallelled " silent monologue " of Marion Bloom occupying the last forty-two pages of the book.

§ V

Hitherto I have given a telegraphic summary of ten of the total of eighteen episodes of *Ulysses*, in order that the plain reader may see how the book runs. I must now compress drastically in order to keep within reasonable limits of space. So here is a tabular statement of the remainder of the work:

TIME.	HOMERIC PARALLEL.	EPISODES IN JOYCE'S " ULYSSES."
4 p.m.	The Sirens	Barmaids' small-talk and a concert at the Ormond bar.
5 p.m.	The Cyclops	Bombastic, drink-inspired discussions by nondescripts in a " pub."

Time.	Homeric Parallel.	Episodes in Joyce's "Ulysses."
8 p.m.	Nausicaa	Gerty MacDowell-Bloom sexual episode at Howth.
10 p.m.	Oxen of the Sun	Delivery of Mina Purefoy of a child in the lying-in hospital.
Midnight	Circe	Stephen Dedalus, and Bloom's drunken orgy in a brothel.
About 12.30 p.m.	Eumæus	Happenings at the cabmen's shelter.
About 2 p.m.	Ithaca	A picking up of loose ends, in the form of question and answer.
About (?)	Penelope	Marion Bloom's "Silent Monologue" in bed.[1]

Bloom wanders in and out of bars, "pub-crawling," and strolls to the Howth Rocks for a breath of fresh air. He sees an attractive girl (a sexual event is realistically exploited), after which he returns to the Holles Street Hospital to await the end of Mrs. Purefoy's confinement. Here he meets Stephen Dedalus carousing with the medical students. The conversation of the party, which includes Buck Mulligan and Haines, is ribald, obscene, and comprehensively obstetric. As they talk the child is born. During the labours we are

[1] The hour is not fixed—the episode is a "fade out" and time disappears.

JAMES JOYCE AND THE PLAIN READER

escorted through a procession of prose-pastiches symbolizing fœtal development and, as Stuart Gilbert informs us, " at first the style is blank (though not wholly devoid of meaning), a lethargic writing up of diplodocan periods which correspond to the reptilian stage of human and embryonic evolution." There is a scrap-heap of Anglo-Saxon words and phrases, a passage in early Church style, and pieces parodying Mandeville and Malory. Then follow parodies of Sir Thomas Browne, the Authorized Bible, Bunyan, Pepys, Swift, Addison, Steele, Sterne, Goldsmith, Burke, Junius, Gibbon, Lamb, De Quincey, Landor, Newman, Pater, Ruskin, and Carlyle, concluding with a hotch-potch of colloquialisms, dialect, and expressive slang. This chapter is a literary *tour de force* and provides an admirable example of Joyce's remarkable sense of language, his craftsmanship, virtuosity, love of words, and the high spirits of which he is capable. The party in merry mood moves off to a neighbouring public-house, where they drink liberally at Stephen's expense. Bloom imbibes sparingly of wine, but Stephen has abandoned all care and deliberately tries to drown unpleasant memories, finally taking to absinthe. From the public-house he goes with Bloom (who has taken to him greatly because he reminds him of his own dead son Rudy) and together they make their way towards the horrid Dublin night-town. With a cry from Stephen of *Introibo ad altare Dei* they enter Mrs. Bella Cohen's bawdy-house in Tyrone Street, and here we come to the truly astounding episode which marks the dramatic climax of the book. Had Joyce nothing but this to his name, it would entitle him to rank as an imaginative writer of great power.

I presume, Mr. plain reader, it has never been your experience to wander in a very drunken state into a Dublin house of ill-fame, so it may be a little difficult for you to appreciate this episode fully unless you are prepared to allow your mind free imaginative flight. You must try to put yourself in the place of the thoroughly soused Stephen and the slightly tipsy, hilarious Bloom who has taken him under his friendly wing. The words Stephen used on entering the brothel indicate his blasphemous, sardonic mood. Once inside, he seems to have lost conscious control of his intelligence: absinthe and the unholy atmosphere of the place help to conjure up all kinds of fantasies, and he is confronted with dreadful hallucinations. Bloom is never so far intoxicated as Stephen; but his mood is sensuous and oriental. In the form of a crazy drama complete with dialogue, asides, and pungent stage directions, Joyce shows us vividly what passes through the minds of the two men in the Tyrone Street inferno. Before the adventure reaches its inevitable end in a brawl, we are given a scenario in which there are preposterous processions of grotesque, magical figures of men, women, animals, and monsters. They utter the wildest gibberings and act the oddest perversities. It is a typhoon of the lowest passions, a horrible nightmare. To appreciate this *Walpurgisnacht* (as it has been aptly called) the episode must be read with complete metaphysical detachment. The sense of reason must at times be allowed to expand enormously, and the mind permitted the utmost licence. Otherwise the intellect reels. Nearly every character, living or dead, in the book is paraded in this mad scene, which in parts transcends all conventional ideas of time, space, and—conventional decency. Granted that the plain reader has the flexibility of mind and the sophistication necessary to enter into the absinthe-poisoned brain of Stephen and that of Bloom, it is by no means difficult to follow. However, a host of perfectly relevant allusions intermixed with the illusions may be missed if some wariness is not exercised.

The psychological treatment of the episode is a direct antecedent of *Work in Progress*,[1] and I think

[1] See Louis Gillet's essay: "James Joyce et son nouveau roman" (*Revue des deux mondes*, 15th August 1931).

that the plain reader may conveniently be informed here that *Dubliners, The Portrait, Ulysses,* and *Work in Progress* are progressive stages in a colossal task which Joyce has set himself: to depict artistically the workings of the human mind in common states or phases of consciousness. In *Dubliners* we are always, except in the story called " The Dead," dealing with the normal conscious minds of commonplace people; in " The Dead " we are taken far into the mysticism of a certain Dublin type. In *The Portrait* we are shown the evolution and growth from childhood to young manhood of a much more important and vital mentality, that of the artist, and not merely a particular artist; for, in a sense, Stephen Dedalus symbolizes the artist generally. In *Ulysses* we are taken *inside* the minds of three standard types: Bloom, the sensual pragmatical materialist; Stephen Dedalus, dreamer, unpractical in a worldly sense, yet highly important to his fellow-creatures; and Marion Bloom, the eternal feminine. In the *Walpurgisnacht* we see the workings of conscious minds which have completely lost all sense of worldly values, with a corresponding loss of control over the stream of consciousness: hence, the deranged imaginings and crackbrained hallucinations. Descriptions of the physical effects of drunkenness are not uncommon, but where, except in *Ulysses*, is there a serious attempt to draw a picture of the psychological turmoils of it?

There is nothing new about attempts to deal with mind-states; literature is full of them. But there are several reasons why we must consider Joyce's attempts to be more successful than most others. He knows his Freud and—his Loyola. He knows what a cesspool the human mind can be, and these two great systematizers have helped to clarify his vision of the subject. It is, in fact, a matter of dispute whether the *Spiritual Exercises* of the Spanish psychologist are less efficacious than those of the Austrian doctor when we wish to purge, cleanse, and disinfect the mental cesspool. Descriptions of mind-processes are rarely convincing; and they seldom approach the lower depths of the subject. Yet those authors who employ the subjective monologue—that is, permit their minds to run free—have probed deeper than the objectivists. Plato, I think, achieves more than Aristotle, Shakespeare and Goethe more than Bacon or Croce, and Dickens more than most of his contemporaries. Plato, Shakespeare, Goethe, and Dickens are, in a sense, the more important forerunners of Joyce in the use of the " Silent Monologue "—for Plato's *Dialogues* are often free monologues or musings interrupted occasionally by dramatic or rhetorical questions; similarly parts of the dialogue of Goethe's *Faust* and of the others. Joyce's perfection of the craftsmanship of the silent monologue, his elimination of the mental "censor" (that is, his complete freedom from psychological repression), and his extraordinary resourcefulness in the employment of language have enabled him to plumb and chart depths of the human psyche that were well known to exist, but were avoided with fear by his predecessors. His art has achieved more than science or theology in presenting those depths.

C. K. Ogden informs us [1] that consciousness is "*the exception rather than the rule in the processes studied by psychology,*" and he says, "most discussions of the unconscious proceed as though there were two distinct realms, the conscious and the unconscious; as when it is said that what is in the unconscious can be brought into consciousness or what is conscious may be repressed into the unconscious." In *Ulysses*, but especially in *Work in Progress*, Joyce also recognizes what Ogden is careful to emphasize, that the working of the mind is not quite so simple as this metaphorical language might indicate. The conscious runs into, and is

[1] *The A B C of Psychology* (Kegan Paul, 1928).

swamped by, the unconscious; and the unconscious obtrudes itself on the conscious. In *Work in Progress* Joyce attempts to show us the mind in the half-conscious state between sleep and waking. At one moment the composite mind with which he is dealing is nearer to waking than to sleep, and then the stream of consciousness of that mind (and the prose descriptive of it) is fairly clear. As soon as there is a lapse into deeper sleep or almost complete unconsciousness, the language becomes turgid, blurred, telescoped, and fantastic. Thus, the myth and story of *Work in Progress* represents an experiment in reducing to language the ebb and flow of the stream of thought between almost unconsciousness and somnolent semi-consciousness. Hence, it is in parts a kind of multi-dimensional emotive narrative capable of a dozen interpretations; or at times—and this is important—*deliberately devoid of any meaning.* It is devoid of meaning in the sense that much music is devoid of meaning, but merely intended to be evocative. The author's other books deal with the alert, conscious mind. This is, without any attempt to qualify or elaborate the terms, the most important unity of all James Joyce's work, and, if the plain reader will but keep it in mind, he may find it helpful in elucidating obscurities.

The immensity of the task of presenting in a few works of art complete pictures of the human mind waking, sleeping, dozing, and under the influence of alcohol, cannot be questioned. The sleep phase has never before been even attempted by any other writer. The question to be settled is: How far has Joyce succeeded in what he has attempted to do? It is one which cannot be fully answered, for we have no standards to help us in the formation of a reasonable judgment on *Work in Progress*. Experimental psychology is still in its infancy, but it is to a well-developed literary branch of the science of psychology of the future we must look chiefly for guidance in regard to the later phase of Joyce's art, if we are to avoid the stupefaction which is so often the companion of appreciation resulting from our merely emotional reactions. Until the science of psychology is well advanced, literary criticism generally must remain what it is—improvisation or guesswork.

The two episodes connecting the *Walpurgisnacht* with Marion Bloom's " silent monologue " show us Stephen being sobered up by Bloom at a cabman's shelter, from which the queer pair go to Bloom's house. The episode in the house is written in a bald catechistic form, ordered, full, and accurate down to the last detail. The same accuracy and orderliness is to be found in the speech and behaviour of the characters, and also in the descriptions of places. In comparison with Joyce's mastery in handling the immense masses of material in *Ulysses*, the work of the best contemporary novelists seems to be greatly inferior.

The final episode, the culminating silent monologue of Marion Bloom (equal in length to one-third of an ordinary novel) has been called a symphony of the universal feminine psyche. It is written without punctuation marks of any kind, and one may say that it has neither beginning nor end. Marion is in bed when Bloom arrives in the bedroom, " reclined semi-laterally, left hand under the head, right leg extended in a straight line and resting on the left leg, flexed, in the attitude of Gea-Tellus, fulfilled, recumbent, big with seed." Not long before she had had a very satisfactory bout with Blazes Boylan; now Bloom suggests that Stephen shall lodge with them, and she likes the idea. Her mind plays round the events of the day, goes over her activities and relations with innumerable servitors and paramours, considers the possibilities in Stephen for amorous amusement; and so forth. It flits like a butterfly from subject to subject, sometimes flies off at strange tangents, but ever returns to the illumination of her all-absorbing sexuality. We are taken boldly inside this woman's very womanly mind. We follow her thoughts wherever they go, and remain with them when they stop to dwell wistfully upon some love adventure or gross experience. Parts of this silent monologue are obscene, as obscene as anything that has ever been written; although the actual space occupied by these obscenities is not great.[1] Imagine their salutary effect upon those whose education has been sheltered—not to mention the prudes and the humbugs! I cannot agree with those critics who assert that *Ulysses* is entirely a clean book, but I should be with them if they said it presents vivid and very complete pictures of the human mind, adding that the human mind has a filthy and unpleasant side, and left it at that. Joyce no more shirks his duty in dealing with the unclean side of the human mind than did the frank and learned casuists of Latin Christianity. But his intention has never that taint of sensuous gloating which constitutes the distinction between scientific description and porno-

[1] I have been told by a friend who is mathematically inclined that if one adds up all the obscene, unspeakable passages of *Ulysses*, the total amounts to less than ten pages out of the 732 in the book—a smaller proportion of obscenity than is to be found in the *Works* of Dr. Francois Rabelais, parish priest of Meudon, now obtainable unexpurgated in the excellent EVERYMAN LIBRARY! *Ulysses* is banned, Rabelais goes free. Does obscenity become clean with age?

JAMES JOYCE AND THE PLAIN READER

graphy. " Joyce's intention," says Valéry Larbaud,[1] " is neither bawdy nor sensual. He merely describes and presents, and in his book (*Ulysses*) the manifestations of the sexual instinct have no more and no less place, and are given neither more nor less importance than, say, pity or scientific curiosity. . . . He has attempted to present man in his integrity : and to do so he has had to take account of the domain of morality, the sexual instinct and its diverse manifestations and perversions ; and, on the physiological side, of the organs of reproduction and their functions." One may well ask why these things are not better left to medical or religious treatises. The answer to this is that Joyce is the natural artist who happens to have had both a Jesuit and a medical training, and the intellectual machinery provided thereby has been utilized in a scientific art remarkable for its controlled vehemence. Religion is one half suppression, whereas art is based upon the principle of expression. Science cares nothing for obscenity. There is little of the sexual in *Ulysses* which was not long ago very well known to the doctors of medicine and of the Church, and Joyce merely goes over the familiar ground once more, using the treasures of Saxon English in forceful expressions often sounding

[1] Introduction to *Gens de Dublin* (Paris, 1926).

obscene to our present over-sensitive ears, rather than obscure the facts in the Latinized English of the pedantic or hypocritical pornographer. We must not lose sight of the fact that the author of *Ulysses* had once been a medical student—and the student of medicine has more opportunities than most other men of observing at close quarters the less pleasant aspects of his fellow-creatures. The medical man has fewer illusions than the layman regarding human nature, and is not inclined to write *ad majorem gloriam hominis*.

Consider the combination of: (*a*) an excellent Jesuit training in grammar, rhetoric, dialectic, philosophy, and psychology, all strengthened by years of close study; (*b*) medical experience; (*c*) great artistic ability. The stream of consciousness of a half-Spanish Dublin sexual athlete, Marion Bloom, as presented by an author with this almost unique set of qualifications becomes, as the woman Rebecca West acknowledges, "one of the most tremendous summations of life that have ever been caught in the net of art"—and this, after her solemn declaration that Mr. Joyce is a great man entirely *without taste*. How lacking in taste is the microscopist who describes the behaviour of, say, the common house-fly, under his instrument !

§ VI

The Italian critic Antonello Gerbi has made a witty statement regarding his reactions to certain authors. When he thinks of Shaw, for example, he says he has a vision of the crackling of minute sparks in the fog of London suburbs, while from Proust there emanates for him a crepuscular fragrance, a distant sweet smell, and from Conrad a wholesome maritime aroma of the warmer gusts of equatorial winds invades and swells his lungs. From the thought of Joyce there issues in slow puffs a mouldy smell of soiled linen, fœtidness of perspiration, of secretions, human skins, and the nauseating acridity of heaving respirations. Gerbi comments: " The cold frenzy to tell *everything,* that fervent, patient, cruel determination to divest himself, to mirror every act, even the most frivolous and ephemeral, in every posture and gesture—all this has in it something of the inhuman." Another critic, Mr. E. M. Foster,[1] having first stated his opinion that *Ulysses* is a " remarkable affair—perhaps the most interesting literary experiment of our day," calls it an " epic of grubbiness and disillusion," and speaks of the " indignation " and " raging " of Joyce. I quote the opinions of these two very intelligent

[1] In *Aspects of the Novel* (Arnold).

writers as representative of mistaken but fairly common feelings in regard to Joyce's work, in which there is no raging or indignation and little or no frenzy, except perhaps in the *Walpurgisnacht* of *Ulysses*. It is, perhaps, pardonable for those who are not acquainted with the Dublin life described by Joyce, to believe that there is behind his terribly objective descriptions a suppressed indignation with the squalor and grubbiness of it all. Here Wyndham Lewis [1] hits the nail on the head when he says that Joyce's mind is not tragic, but genial and comic. The bulk of *Ulysses* and also of *Work in Progress* is *essentially* comical and humorous, with an element of the sardonic permeating the former, but not the latter. Indeed, a good case could be made out to show that each of Joyce's works is more genial than its predecessors. But there is more to the matter than that, and we shall get still closer to its core if we consider Joyce's idea of the aim of the novel as akin to Synge's idea of drama—that it should be symphonic. " The drama," writes Synge in the preface to *The Tinker's Wedding*, " does not teach or prove anything. Analysts with their problems, and teachers with their systems, are soon as old-fashioned as the pharmacopœia of Galen . . . the best plays of Ben Jonson and Molière can no

[1] *Time and Western Man* (Chatto & Windus).

more go out of fashion than the blackberries on the hedges." Synge also says that, of the things which nourish the imagination, humour is the most helpful. Who can doubt it? These principles underlie *Ulysses* which, as regards humour, bears some resemblance to Swift's Lilliput, the most genial of the Dean's works. Joyce is Gulliver looking down upon the Dublin-Lilliputians Bloom, Dedalus, Marion, Buck Mulligan, and the others whose minds and activities are, when micro-scopically examined, shown to us as trifling, comical, and very human affairs. In Swift's Lilliput there is no *sæva indignatio*, but merely a close account of human foibles and frailties. And so also in *Ulysses*. This is perhaps the only resemblance between Swift's work and that of Joyce; as regards craftsmanship there is none. Swift is direct in statement and politically minded. As regards the craft of writing, his simple sovereign rule is " the right words in the right places." His political and social influence has been immense, for was it not he who two hundred years ago stimulated the Irish into the movement which in our own time became Sinn Fein and ended in the establishment of the Irish Free State? Joyce's political or social in-fluence is and must always be negligible, because of the " symphonic " quality of his work, but his literary craftsmanship already provides endless stimulation and inspiration to writers of diverse nationalities—indeed it is difficult to discuss the contemporary novel without taking account of his influence. One might argue that if (outside the literary art) Joyce exerts any influence upon human behaviour, it is an evil one, because he has given us vivid and terrible pictures of human vileness. This is one of the reactions of sensitive minds that have been subjected to an over-intensive religious education, with its lacerating self-analysis; a process which has often a devastating effect upon whatever spirit of charity and tolerance may have been born in an individual. There is always a risk that it may engender a sadistic side to one's mentality: but Joyce is saved from this by the natural geniality and extreme sophistication which, after *The Portrait* period, dominate his works. In *Ulysses* and in *Work in Progress* we find religion regarded with a whimsical and tolerant comicality which is never mocking in the sense that Anatole France is mocking in, say, *La Rôtisserie de la Reine Pedauque*. *The Portrait* stands by itself, in that the imaginative picture of evil is not redeemed by geniality. It was a fearful, brooding, and sadly disturbed man who wrote it.

To Wyndham Lewis's work, already mentioned,

I would refer the plain reader who wishes to read something about the time-aspect of *Ulysses*. I do not pretend to have any clear concept of Time, except that symbolized by a straight line which stretches with a shimmer both ways into infinity. On the whole, Joyce follows the line. But one must never forget that he loves to wander, physically and spiritually. Often he plays with Time, telescoping or expanding events or, as in the *Walpurgisnacht*, jumping into what Mr. Dunne [1] would call "other planes"; or, as in *Work in Progress*, making it an Einsteinian time-space; or on occasion, juggling with the relations of cause and effect, as I understand human reason is now permitted to do by Schrödinger. He inclines towards the ideas of Gianbattista Vico, and practises them. The metaphysician will find ample apparatus in Joyce upon which to practise intellectual acrobatics; the rest of us had better pass on. We must be content with the story, not in Mr. Edgar Wallace's sense of this word, but the psychological fable which is far more thrilling, more elevating, more flattering, and more beneficial to human nature than the average Wallacian product. Joyce never idealizes vice and criminality by throwing a romantic glamour round it, as Wallace has done, and as most criminal

[1] In *An Experiment with Time*.

authors do. Through the Irishman's eyes evil appears thoroughly, even sentimentally vile; and never otherwise. It would be interesting to compare with, say, *On the Spot*, a work written by a Joyce who had been persuaded to spend a few weeks in Chicago. I doubt if it would be so highly praised by the gangsters, criminal or literary.

It is customary in an essay of this sort to attempt a summing up as the end approaches, and to offer a series of conclusions. I propose to avoid both, as I hope that what has gone before is sufficiently explicit in itself; and I am not so cocksure of my opinions as to tabulate them and to write Q.E.D. underneath. There is no author living whose works are more difficult to survey, appraise, and criticize; and much of what I have said must be considered as a selection and piecing together of ideas expressed by others, to which I have added some of my own. The greatest problem with which Joycean criticism is confronted is *Work in Progress*, and, as regards this piece of emotive writing, all the critics are at sea. For all we know, it may yet prove to be the perfectly expressed history of man. It is impossible yet to say whether it is an experiment of the highest importance for the future of language, literature, and psychology; whether it symbolizes the running to seed of a great mind;

whether it is a vast joke; or whether it is the application to prose of a new theory in musical notation![1]

Valéry Larbaud suggests (and he is one of Joyce's most ardent admirers) that *Work in Progress* is an abuse of language. In it Joyce seems to be doing in his sphere something akin to what Gertrude Stein has already done in hers. This American writer has pushed dissociation from Time so far that the result is nearly always meaningless except to herself; and Joyce is identifying himself with time-space so closely that he has to assist a group of translators who attempt to make something of *Anna Livia* in another language. *Work in Progress* is ingenious, but so are Volapük and Esperanto; and some may consider them more beautiful as languages than Joyce's remarkable experiment, though neither of them has its rhythm or its spaciousness.

Let us return to the point of departure and consider for a moment *Anna Livia*, of which this is a passage:

" Don Dom Dombdomb and his wee follyo! Was his help inshored in the Stork and Pelican against bungelars, 'flu, and third party risks?

[1] See an article, "On Hearing James Joyce," by A. T. Cunninghame, in *The Modern Scot*, vol. ii., No. 3 October 1931.

I heard he dug good tin with his doll when he raped her home, Sabrine asthore, in a parakeet's cage, by dredgerous lands and devious delts, playing carched and mythed with the gleam of her shadda, past auld min's manse, and maisons Allfou and the rest of incurables and the last of immurables, the quaggy waag for stumbling."

In the French version this becomes:

" Dom Dom Dommdomb et elvette sa mie. Est-ce qu'il assura son aide chez Cigogne-Pélican contre Boupilleurs, glippe et tiers périlleux? Il parait qu'enlevée il la bel et bien fouilla, sa Sabrine saumoureuse, dans une cage de perruche boitant par les lyses, faux-filant par deltas, jouant shah que pelotte les reflets de son ombre pres Vils Viellard et Maisons-Alfou et Issy-le-Repos et Alta l'Oubliette surlaroutant viers lou capilot."

Now whatever we may think of the rhythm or the reason or the emotive value of either, one effect is produced by both. Laughter. I confess I have failed in my attempts to discover exactly what I am laughing at as I read parts of *Anna Livia* and *Anna Livie*; I cannot say for certain whether it was at the linguistic incongruities or at the comical underlying ideas. There seems to be a slightly stronger satiric flavour about the French than about the English, though a satiric flavour is often inherent in the French language, and need not be conscious in the writer. This is sometimes very obvious as, for example, in the French version of Mrs. Baker Eddy's masterpiece. I have recently read *Science et Santé avec la clef des écritures,* and there were times when I thought I was reading the *Dictionnaire Philosophique* of Voltaire, or the musings of that very human fictitious character, the Abbé Jérome Coignard.

Work in Progress is entirely genial in conception; even those parts which we do not understand may evoke laughter. Is it then a huge joke, a *practical* joke? The solemn joke, a difficult literary exercise, is by no means uncommon amongst Irish authors, most of whom are playboys at heart; it would be nothing new for one of them to indulge his fancy in a grand bravura creation, especially if he be a man of Joyce's geniality and ability. Has the dreadfully serious young man of the verse and *The Portrait* mellowed into a Herculean playboy in his middle age? Is *Work in Progress* a superb piece of nonsense-prose springing from that " gigantism of Irishness " which I have mentioned already?—an item flung at the heads of critics, a breed very heartily detested by Joyce. This, after all, may prove to be for some plain readers quite a reasonable as well as the simplest explanation of it. I offer it chiefly because, so far as I am aware, it has not occurred to any one else to mention it; and I offer it as only *one* of the many possible explanations. It will, at all events, stand on its legs—which is more than some of the others can do.

Besides, it may provide the plain reader with an idea to replace that conclusion which I have hitherto most carefully avoided. For *Work in Progress*, notwithstanding its complexity, *is* a magnificent piece of Rabelaisian, laughter-provoking literature, whatever else we may say about it.

APPENDIX

(A) Bibliography of the Works of James Joyce

1. *Chamber Music.* (Poems, 1907.) Now published by Jonathan Cape Ltd.
2. *Dubliners.* (Short Stories, 1914.) Now published by Jonathan Cape Ltd.
3. *A Portrait of the Artist as a Young Man.* (Novel, 1916.) Now published by Jonathan Cape Ltd.
4. *Exiles.* (A Play in three Acts, 1918.) Now published by Jonathan Cape Ltd.
5. *Ulysses.* (A Novel, 1922.) Published by Shakespeare & Co., Paris, and sold at Sylvia Beach's Bookshop. (The sale of the English edition of *Ulysses* is forbidden in England. Am I right in believing that there is no legal obstacle to the sale of *Ulysse*, the French translation, by MM. A. Morel, Stuart Gilbert, Valéry Larbaud, and James Joyce (Ed. Adrienne Monnier and J.-O. Fourcade, 1929)? This French version is a *tour de force*, and can be strongly recommended.)
6. *Work in Progress.* (I should call this a poetic novel.) First published in *transition*, Nos. 1-20 (1927-30).
7. *Anna Livia Plurabelle.* (Third version of an extract from *Work in Progress.*) Published by Faber & Faber.

JAMES JOYCE AND THE PLAIN READER

8. *Haveth Childers Everywhere.* (Extract from *Work in Progress.*) Published by Faber & Faber, 1931.
9. *Work in Progress.* Published by Faber & Faber, 1932.
10. Note also the *Bibliography* of Joyce's Works by Dr. Jacob Schwartz. Published by The Ulysses Press Ltd., 1932.

N.B.—The above rough-and-ready list is a bibliography for the use of the *plain reader*, and not for the bibliophile, who is advised to examine item No. 10.

(B) CRITICISM, ARTICLES, ETC., FOR THE PLAIN READER WHO WOULD LIKE TO BECOME BETTER ACQUAINTED WITH THE IMPORTANCE AND IMPLICATIONS OF JOYCE'S WORKS.

1. *James Joyce: His First Forty Years.* By Herbert S. Gorman (Geoffrey Bles, 1926). This book gives a general account of Joyce's life and works up to and including *Ulysses.* It also contains a bibliography and a list of articles on Joyce.
2. *Scrutinies,* Vol. 1. By Various Authors. Contains an essay on Joyce.
3. *Axel's Castle.* By Edmund Wilson. (Scribner's.)
4. *The Criterion,* No. 1. Contains an English version of Valéry Larbaud's penetrating review of *Ulysses.*
5. *Our Examination round his Factification for Incamination of Work in Progress.* Various writers expound different aspects of *Work in Progress.* (Shakespeare & Co., Paris, 1929.)

APPENDIX

6. *Ulysses*: A Study. By Stuart Gilbert. (Faber & Faber, 1930.) This is a detailed exposition of *Ulysses*, with many extracts. It is the best substitute for the original.

N.B.—The reader is also referred to the works mentioned in the footnotes to the present essay, especially to Wyndham Lewis's *Time and Western Man,* Louis Gillet's essays in the *Revue des deux Mondes* of 1st June 1925 and 15th June 1931, and to the essay by M. Daniel-Rops (*Le monologue intérieur*) in *Le Correspondant,* 25th January 1932. Criticism and commentary on Joyce is becoming voluminous, but the above list contains, in my opinion, the most interesting that has appeared hitherto.

THE END